In The Wild

Cheetahs

Stephanie St. Pierre

Heinemann Library
Chicago, Illinois

D1317132

Customer Service 888-454-2279

Visit our website at www.heinemannlibrary.com

Designed by Depke Design
Printed in China

12 11 10 09
10 9 8 7 6 5

Library of Congress Cataloging-in-Publication Data
St. Pierre, Stephanie.
   Cheetahs / Stephanie St. Pierre.
      p. cm. -- (In the wild)
Includes bibliographical references (p.   ).
   ISBN 1-58810-106-1 (lib. bdg.)   ISBN 1-58810-379-X (pbk. bdg.)
   ISBN 978-1-58810-106-8 (lib. bdg.)   ISBN 978-1-58810-379-6 (pbk. bdg.)
   1. Cheetah--Juvenile literature. [1. Cheetah.] I. Title. II. Series.
QL737.C23 S68 2001
599.75'9--dc21
                                                                00-012651

Acknowledgments
The author and publishers are grateful to the following for permission to reproduce copyright material:
Kevin Schafer/Corbis, p. 4 (far right); Cyndy Conger/Corbis, p. 4, (center); George Lepp/Corbis, p. 4, (far left); The Purcell Team/Corbis, pp. 5, 6, 9; Nicole Duplaix/Corbis, p. 7; W. Perry Conway/Corbis, p. 8; Tom Brakefield/Corbis, pp. 10, 11, 12, 13, 18, 20, 23; Yann Arthus-Bertrand/Corbis, pp. 14, 19; Mitch Reardon/Photo Researchers Inc., pp. 15, 17; Carl Ammann/Corbis, p. 16; Picture Press/Corbis, p. 21; Mary Ann McDonald/Corbis, p. 22.

Cover photograph: W. Perry Conway/Corbis

Some words are shown in bold, **like this.** You can find out what they mean by looking in the glossary.

Contents

Cheetah Relatives 4

Where Cheetahs Live 6

The Family 8

Running 10

Hunting 12

Eating 14

Babies 16

Playing 18

Growing Up 20

Cheetah Facts 22

Glossary 24

More Books to Read 24

Index 24

Cheetah Relatives

Cheetahs are a kind of cat. All cats belong to a family called **felines.** All of the animals shown on this page are felines.

leopard

cougar

house cat

Felines have sharp teeth and claws used for hunting and eating meat.

All cats like to keep clean. They wash their faces with their paws. Cats have scratchy tongues they use to **groom** themselves.

Where Cheetahs Live

Cheetahs live in the **grasslands** of Africa. They like fields with tall grasses and small trees they can hide behind when they are hunting.

The pattern of black spots on the cheetah's coat is a good **camouflage.** This helps the cheetah to hide from other animals.

The Family

Grown **female** cheetahs live alone until they have babies. They travel and hunt over very large areas of land. Babies stay with their mother until they are about two years old.

Adult **male** cheetahs live and hunt together in small groups. These groups are often made up of male **littermates.**

Running

The cheetah is the fastest runner of all animals. It can run as fast as a car speeding along the highway. The cheetah does not run for fun but to hunt other speedy animals.

It takes only a few seconds for a cheetah to reach its full speed, but it gets tired quickly. A chase usually lasts less than one minute.

Hunting

Cheetahs hunt during the day. Antelope, zebra, hares, and wildebeest are their **prey.** The cheetah **stalks** its prey, getting as close as possible. Then it runs.

If the cheetah is close enough to its prey when
the chase starts, it will be a successful hunt.
The cheetah bites its prey on the neck, killing
it quickly.

Eating

After a hunt the cheetah is often too tired to eat. Sometimes it will hide its **kill** and rest until it is ready to eat.

Sometimes it does not get the chance to eat at all. Lions or hyenas will steal the cheetah's kill if they can.

Babies

Cheetahs usually have three to five cubs in a **litter.** Cubs are very fluffy until they are about four months old. They keep a fluffy **mane** until they are one year old.

Cheetah mothers must protect their babies from enemies, like lions and caracals. But sometimes cheetah cubs are killed while their mothers are away hunting.

Playing

Like all cats, Cheetahs are curious. Young cheetahs will sniff and paw at strange things. Is this something to eat? Is it something to hunt? The cheetah wants to know.

Cheetahs like to climb trees. Sometimes they climb to get a better view. Sometimes they climb to find a nice place to nap.

Growing Up

Cheetahs must learn to hunt before they can leave their mothers. At first, they practice hunting by playing. Sometimes they pretend to hunt each other. Later they hunt small animals, like rabbits.

After a hard day of playing and hunting, cheetah cubs **groom** each other. Grown-up cheetahs also groom each other after they hunt.

Cheetah Facts

- Cheetahs do not roar, but they can purr. They can also **yelp** and make a kind of chirping sound.

• The Cheetah's long tail helps it to balance
and turn. It also has thick lined pads on the
bottom of its paws that help it keep on track
at high speeds.

Glossary

camouflage pattern or color that helps an animal hide easily
felines family of animals that includes all kinds of cats
female girl or woman
grassland large area of grass with few trees
groom to clean and smooth fur
kill dead animal to be eaten
litter group of animals born at the same time
littermates one of a group of babies born at the same time
male boy or man
mane long hair that grows around the head and shoulders of an animal
prey animals hunted for food
stalk to watch and carefully follow
yelp to make a crying sound

Index

babies 8, 16–17
cats 4, 5, 18
eating 5, 14–15
enemies 15, 17
feline 4, 5
grooming 5, 21

hunting 5, 6, 8, 9, 10, 12–13, 14, 20, 21
making sounds 22
running 10–11, 12, 13, 14
stalking 12

More Books to Read

MacMillan, Dianne. *Cheetahs*. Minneapolis, Minn.: Lerner Publishing Co., 1997.

Morrison, Taylor. *Cheetah*. New York: Henry Holt & Company, 1998.

Welsbacher, Anne. *Cheetahs*. Minneapolis, Minn.: Abdo Publishing Co., 2000.

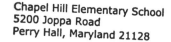

Chapel Hill Elementary School
5200 Joppa Road
Perry Hall, Maryland 21128

24